Snow White
and the Seven Dwarfs

Retold by Jenny Giles
Illustrated by Pat Reynolds

NELSON PRICE MILBURN

Once upon a time, a King and Queen lived in a grand castle with their beautiful young daughter, Snow White.

But when Snow White was still a child, her mother died, and some years later her father married again.

The new Queen was very vain, and she spent many hours in front of her magic mirror. Every day, she would ask it,
*"Mirror, mirror, on the wall,
Who is the fairest one of all?"*

And the mirror would always reply,
*"The Queen who lives in the castle grand
Is the fairest one in all the land."*

The Queen was delighted to hear this.

3

As the years went by,
Snow White became
more and more beautiful.

One day, when the Queen asked,
*"Mirror, mirror, on the wall,
Who is the fairest one of all?"*
the mirror replied,
*"Snow White who lives in the castle grand
Is now the fairest in the land."*

The Queen was very angry.
She ordered a huntsman
to take Snow White
deep into the forest and kill her.

But the huntsman could not hurt
the beautiful Princess.
"Run!" he said to her.
"Run away and never return,
or the wicked Queen will kill you."

5

Snow White ran through the forest.
She was all alone, and very frightened.
Then, just as she was beginning
to think she was lost forever,
she saw a little cottage among the trees.

Snow White opened the door and went in.
Everything inside the cottage was so tiny!

Along one wall
there were seven little beds.

On the table there were seven little plates and seven little cups.
There were also seven little chairs, and each bed, plate, cup and chair was a different colour.

The room was not very tidy, so Snow White washed the little dishes and swept the floor.

By this time, Snow White was very tired. She lay down to rest on one of the beds, and she was soon asleep.

Some time later, the seven little men who lived in the cottage came home. They were dwarfs, and each was dressed in a different colour.

"Look!" said the Red Dwarf.
"Our door is open!"

"The floor has been swept!" said the Orange Dwarf.

"Who can this be, asleep on my bed?" asked the Yellow Dwarf.

Their voices awoke Snow White.
She sat up and looked at the dwarfs
in surprise.
The dwarfs stared back at Snow White.
They had never seen anyone so beautiful.

Snow White told the dwarfs
why she had come to their cottage.

"You must never go back to that
wicked Queen," said the Green Dwarf.

"You must stay here,"
said the Brown Dwarf.

"We will take care of you,"
said the Blue Dwarf.

The dwarfs made a beautiful bed
for Snow White, and they found a cup
and plate for her.

Every day, they went off to work
down in the mines, and Snow White
took care of the cottage for them.
"Do not ever answer the door to anyone,"
said the Purple Dwarf,
as they left each morning.

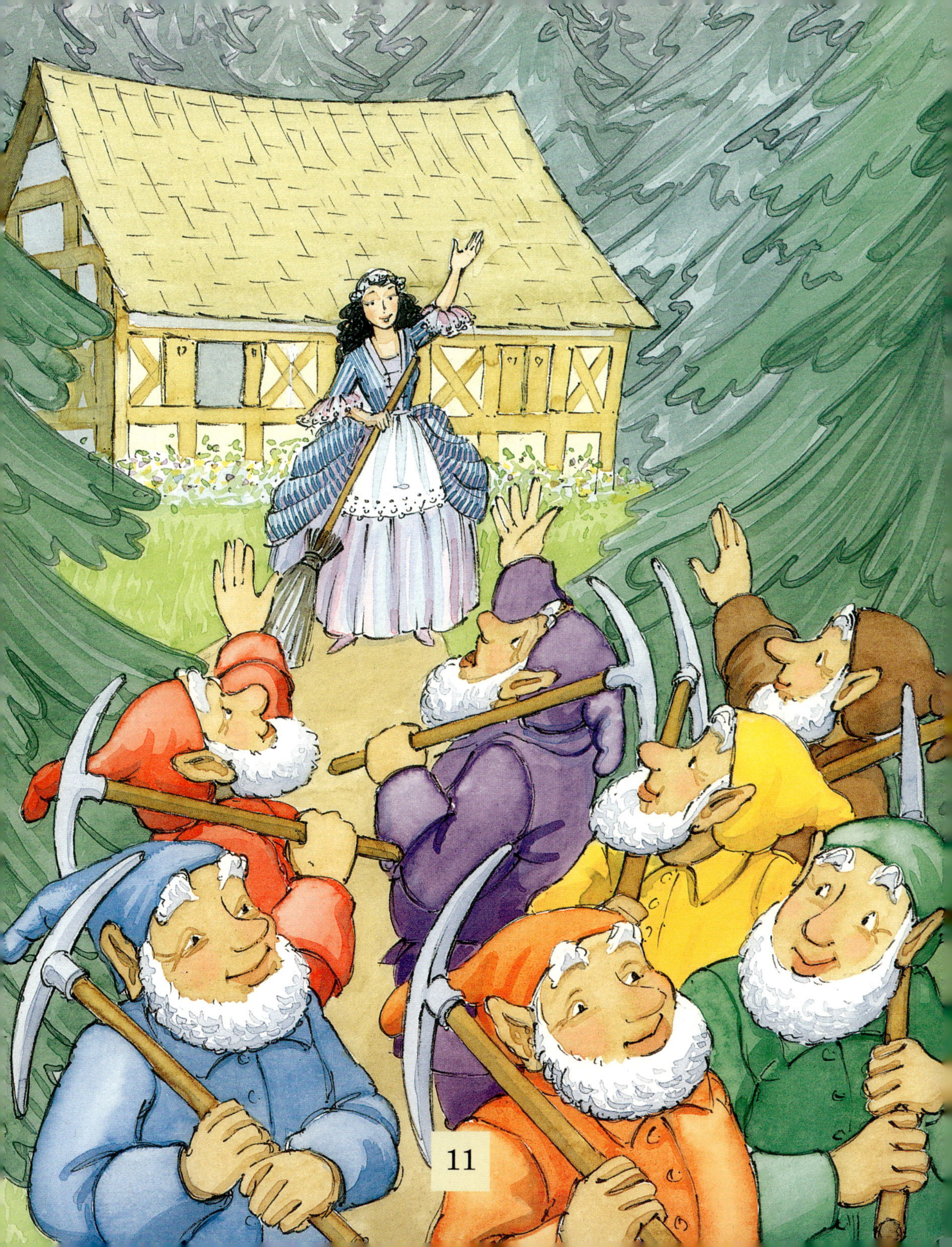

Then one day, when the wicked Queen
spoke to her magic mirror, it replied,
"Snow White who lives
With the dwarfs in the wood
Is the fairest of all.
She is kind and good."

The Queen was furious
when she heard this, and she thought
of a plan to kill Snow White.
She took a basket of apples
and filled one apple with poison.
Then she disguised herself
as an old woman
and went to the dwarfs' cottage.
"Apples! Apples for sale!" she called.

Snow White remembered
that she must not open the door,
so she looked out the window.

The apples looked delicious.
Snow White reached out her hand,
and the wicked Queen gave her
the poisoned apple.

At the first bite, Snow White
fell to the floor in a deep sleep.
The Queen chuckled to herself,
and returned to the castle.

That night, when the dwarfs came home,
they found Snow White on the floor.

"Oh! What has happened?"
cried the Red Dwarf.

"Our beautiful Princess is dead!"
cried the Orange Dwarf.

"We will put Snow White on her bed,"
said the Yellow Dwarf.

"And we will make a glass cover to go
over her," said the Green Dwarf.

"Let us carry her up to the hillside,"
said the Brown Dwarf.

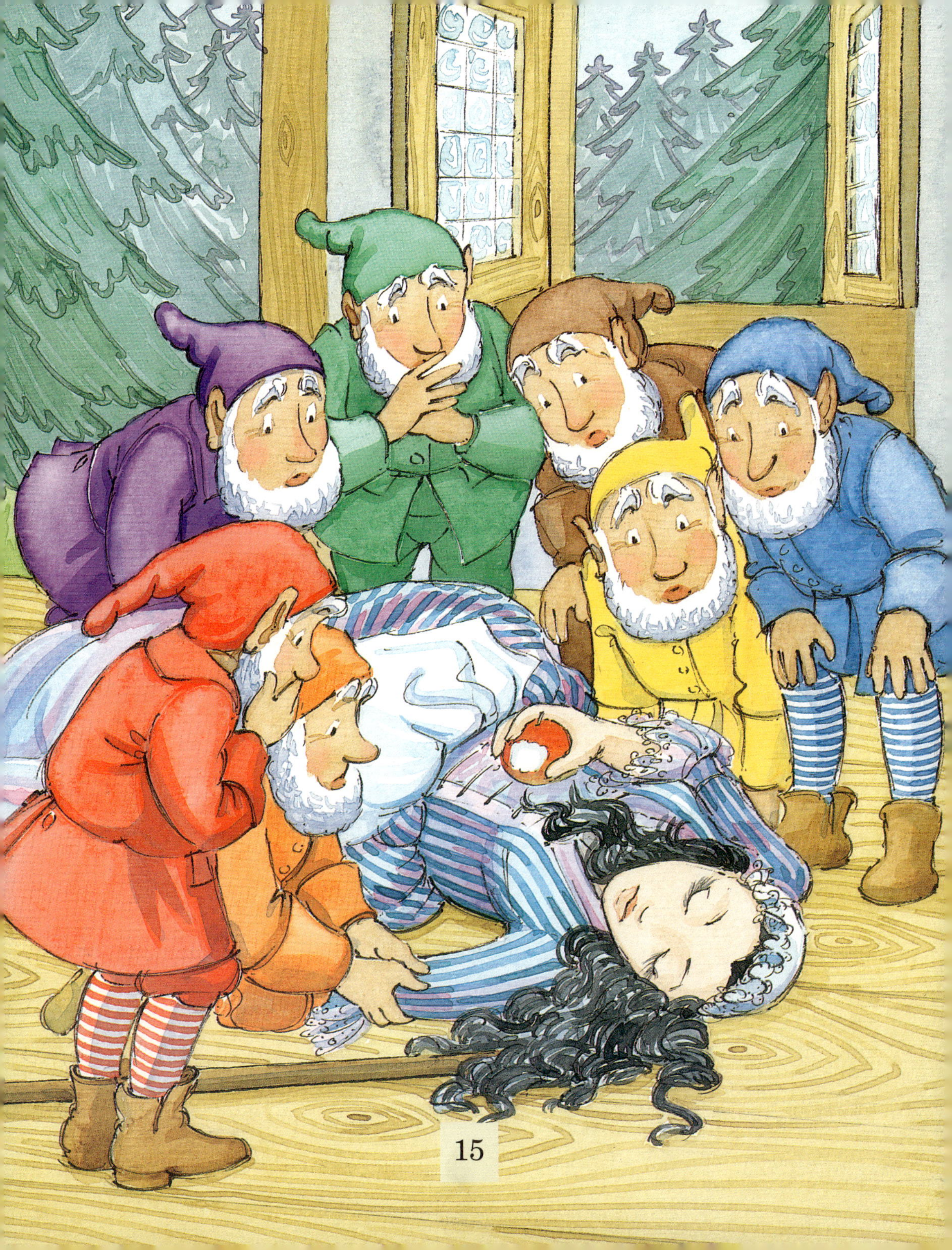

"We will all take turns to watch over her," said the Blue Dwarf.

"Here lies Snow White," said the Purple Dwarf.

One day, a Prince came riding by.
He was amazed to see Snow White.
"This beautiful Princess should be in a palace," he said. "Let her come home with me."

The dwarfs did not want to lose Snow White, but at last they agreed to let her go.

Then, just as the Prince's servants
were lifting Snow White up,
the piece of apple fell out of her mouth.
She awoke from her deep sleep
and saw the handsome Prince.

At exactly the same moment,
far away in the castle,
the magic mirror fell off the wall
and killed the wicked Queen.

The dwarfs were delighted
that their beloved Snow White was alive again,
and they knew in their hearts
that she would be happy with the Prince.

19

The dwarfs waved goodbye to Snow White.
"I will come and visit you!"
she called to them.

Snow White and the Prince were married, and they lived happily ever after.

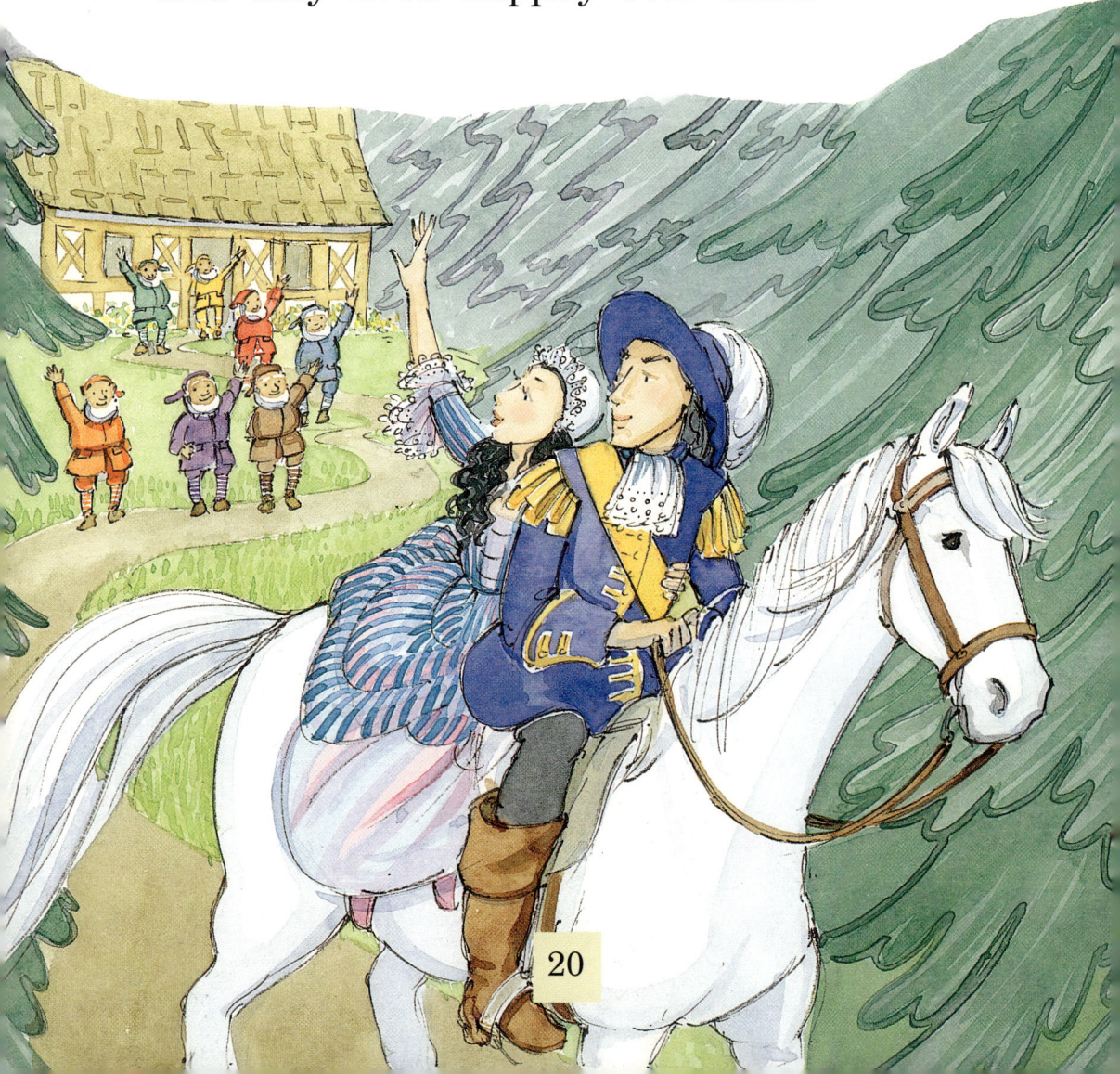

A play
Snow White
and the Seven Dwarfs

People in the play

	Reader		Red Dwarf
	Snow White		Orange Dwarf
	Queen		Yellow Dwarf
	Mirror		Green Dwarf
	Huntsman		Brown Dwarf
	Prince		Blue Dwarf
	Prince's Servants (mime only)		Purple Dwarf

Reader

Once upon a time, a King and Queen
lived in a grand castle
with their beautiful daughter, Snow White.
But when Snow White was still a child,
her mother died, and some years later
her father married again.
The new Queen was very vain,
and she spent many hours
in front of her magic mirror.
Every day, she would ask it:

Queen

*Mirror, mirror, on the wall,
Who is the fairest one of all?*

Mirror

*The Queen who lives in the castle grand
Is the fairest one in all the land.*

Queen

I am the most beautiful woman
in the land. Oh, I am so delighted!

Reader

But as the years went by,
Snow White became
more and more beautiful.
One day, when the Queen asked:

Queen

Mirror, mirror, on the wall,
Who is the fairest one of all?

Reader

The mirror replied to the Queen:

Mirror

Snow White who lives in the castle grand
Is now the fairest in the land.

Reader

The Queen was very angry.
She ordered a huntsman to take Snow White deep into the forest and kill her.

Huntsman

You must come with me, Snow White.
The Queen wants me to take you
into the forest.

Reader

Snow White went with the huntsman.

Snow White

I don't like it here in the forest.
Please take me home.

Huntsman

I can't take you home.
The wicked Queen will kill you.
Run! Run away and never return.

Reader

Snow White ran through the forest.
She was all alone, and very frightened.

Snow White

I can see a cottage among the trees.
I wonder who lives there?

Reader

Snow White opened the door
of the cottage, and went in.

Snow White

What a lovely room!
But everything in it is so tiny!
There are seven little beds, seven little chairs,
seven little plates and cups,
all in different colours!
But this room is not very tidy!
I will wash the dishes and sweep the floor.

Reader

Snow White was very tired.
She fell asleep on one of the beds.
Some time later, the seven dwarfs
who lived in the cottage came home.
They were dressed in different colours.

Red Dwarf

Look! Our door is open!

Orange Dwarf

The floor has been swept!

Yellow Dwarf

Who can this be, asleep on my bed?

Reader

Their voices awoke Snow White.
She sat up and looked at the dwarfs.
The dwarfs stared back at Snow White.
They had never seen anyone so beautiful.

Snow White

I am a Princess, and I have been sent away from the Palace.
The wicked Queen made the huntsman bring me into the forest.
I was lost until I came to your cottage.

Green Dwarf

You can't go back to the wicked Queen!

Brown Dwarf

You must stay here.

Blue Dwarf

We will take care of you.

Reader

The dwarfs made a bed for her,
and gave her a cup and plate.
Every day, they went off to work,
and Snow White took care of the cottage.

Purple Dwarf

Do not ever answer the door
to anyone while we are away.

Reader

Then one day, far away in the castle,
the magic mirror said to the Queen:

Mirror

Snow White who lives
With the dwarfs in the wood
Is the fairest of all.
She is kind and good.

Queen

I cannot believe this!
I must think of a plan to kill Snow White.
I will fill an apple with poison,
and take it to her in the forest.

Reader

The Queen took a basket of apples and filled one apple with poison. Then, disguised as an old woman, she went to the dwarfs' cottage.

Queen

Apples! Apples for sale.

Snow White

Oh, those apples look so delicious! Please let me have one.

Queen

Here is the juiciest apple of all.

Reader

At the first bite of the apple, Snow White fell to the floor in a deep sleep.

Queen

Ha! Ha! Ha! Snow White is dead, and now I am the most beautiful woman in the land again.

Reader

When the dwarfs came home,
they saw Snow White lying on the floor.

Red Dwarf

Oh! What has happened?

Orange Dwarf

Our beautiful Princess is dead!

Yellow Dwarf

We will put Snow White on her bed.

Green Dwarf

We will make a glass cover to go over her.

Brown Dwarf

Let us carry her up to the hillside.

Blue Dwarf

We will all take turns to watch over her.

Purple Dwarf

Here lies Snow White.

Reader

Then one day, a Prince came riding by. He was amazed to see Snow White.

Prince

This beautiful Princess should be in a palace. Let her come home with me.

Reader

The dwarfs did not want to lose her,
but at last they agreed to let Snow White
go with the Prince.

Then, just as the Prince's servants
were lifting Snow White up,
the piece of apple fell out of her mouth.
She awoke from her deep sleep
and saw the handsome Prince.

At exactly the same moment,
far away in the castle,
the magic mirror fell off the wall
and killed the wicked Queen.

Dwarfs (all together)

Our beloved Snow White is alive again!

Reader

Snow White and the Prince were married,
and they lived happily ever after.